Mindful Me Goes to Sleep by Erin LeDrew
and Illustrated by Stephanie Mackay

Published by
Three Favourite Things

For permissions contact: threefavouritethings.ca

Cover by Stephanie Mackay

ISBN 978-1-7932-0662-6

MINDFUL ME GOES TO SLEEP

A bedtime routine based on mindfulness.

For Ben and Katie

May you always feel like
you can conquer worry.

You had a
LONG day,
and you need to recharge
your **heart**
Here's a good place
where we both should start...

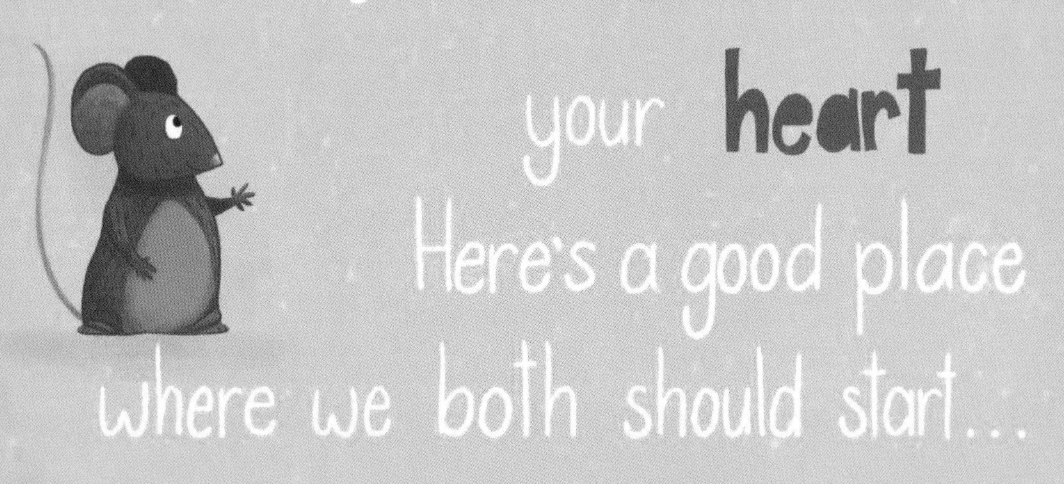

Lay down flat on the
Floor
with your feet
UP the wall.

2
3
Take three deep breaths.
Don't let your legs fall.

Now
TAP
between your
eyebrows,
and move
Flat
on your
back.

Focus on your **Breath**,

and **NOT** on the things you lack.

BEND
your knees
and
put your feet on the floor.

STOMP out all of your **feelings**, whatever they are.

Move your hands to your **CHEEKS** and **slow** down your thoughts.

Focus on your Breathing,
and not Thinking a lot.

Place one hand
to your **mouth**,
and let kind words **flow**
Our language is **POWERFUL**,
as you already know.

I am strong

Find

1. three
2. favourite
3. things

about your day.

GRATITUDE
is
IMPORTANT,
practice it
everyday.

Place one hand
on your Heart
and move the other
to your tummy.

Press DOWN
good and strong like
you're SQUEEZING
your mommy.

Close your eyes and picture
the **BEST DAY EVER.**
When you wake, I hope you'll feel
ready to discover.

ALL IS WELL,
NOW IT'S
TIME TO REST.

Give yourself a big hug,
you're doing your best.

Mindful Me practices.

For those of you interested in the practices behind the actions:

Laying with your legs up the wall is based on Yoga and Mindfulness and has been shown to slow down the heart rate and provide a calming sensation.

Tapping between your eyebrows is based on the Emotional Freedom Technique.

Laying flat on the floor is a Yoga pose known as Shavasana. It has many benefits and can be used as a Grounding Technique.

Stomping out your feelings is a purposeful pairing of Visualization (thoughts/feelings/emotions) and a Physical action to release.

Bringing attention to the words in your head is an act of Mindfulness and brings awareness to the importance of choosing our words carefully.

Finding three favourite things is a practice of Gratitude.

Placing your hand on your heart and belly is a Yoga Mindfulness practice.

Picturing the future on your own terms is a powerful strategy known as Visualization. It is a common practice used with Athletes.

The final practice is self-care

Erin LeDrew

Erin LeDrew has been a Recreation Therapist at Canada's largest mental health and addiction teaching hospital for over a decade. During that time she became a wife and mother and she has always called Toronto, Canada home. Erin's passion for creative expression has lead to many of her endeavors including writing this book. Based on her years of working in the mental health field, Erin understands there is a strong need for people to learn how to be well, and stay well, from a young age.

Stephanie Mackay

Stephanie Mackay is a freelance visual artist/graphic designer specializing in children's illustrations. Six years ago, Stephanie made the decision to go back to school to pursue her dream of illustrating children's books. Since graduating from the Illustration & Design program at Dawson College in 2016, she has illustrated seven children's books. Her goal is to make people smile, one image at a time.

Printed in Great Britain
by Amazon